Online $uccess can be yours

Small Business

Double your business o...

If you're a business owner or manager, this book i... no technical jargon or HTML code. Instead, you'll ... tested techniques that will help you grow your bus... offline!

Each tactic is restricted to one page or less. In just 15 minutes a day, you'll find a wealth of techniques you can use to

- increase your sales of products and services
- raise your credibility and visibility online
- boost the traffic to your site
- provide better service and support
- expand your use of effective online business practices

Your customers and prospects will *experience* the difference!

> *This is a terrific book! Every one of these tactics is profitable and something you can either do or start right away.*
> -David Garfinkel, author
> Advertising Headlines That Make You Rich

> *This book cuts through the hype and provides well-organized, easy-to-follow, bite-sized tasks for building your online business. It's an easy, pleasurable read with lots of real-world examples.*
> -Joshua Feinberg, MCSE, Small Business Technology Expert

> *Wow! This book is packed with easily implemented online branding and marketing technique...* ...couldn't put it
> *down. A real winner for...*
> -Mellan... ...iness Strategies

If you're ready to take the next step in expanding your online business, get started *now*!

ISBN 1-931838-04-6

51495

9 781931 838047

$14.95

Y0-AGD-760

POL6705Z7

Online $uccess Tactics

101 Ways to Build Your Small Business

Jeanette S. Cates, PhD

Twin Towers Press - Austin, Texas

Online Success Tactics
101 Ways to Build Your Small Business
By Jeanette S. Cates

Published by
Twin Towers Press
10502 Hardrock
Austin, TX 78750-2037 U.S.A.
orders@twintowerspress.com
http://www.TwinTowersPress.com

Unattributed quotations by Jeanette S. Cates

Printed in the United States of America

Library of Congress Control Number: 2001119798

Ebook version ISBN 1-931838-03-8
Paperback version ISBN 1-931838-04-6
Hardcover version ISBN 1-931838-05-4

Layout by Vicki Bass, http://www.VickiBass.com
Cover Design by Vaughan Davidson, http://www.KillerCovers.com

Dedication

To Mother for your loving encouragement in so many ways
and
To Bob who continues to trust and believe in the dream.
Thank you!

Acknowledgements

Every book is a collaborative effort. This book was inspired by the work of Paul Montelongo, in his book *101 Power Strategies: Tools to Promote Yourself as the Contractor of Choice*. His clear ideas and easy-to-read format led the way. His encouragement and friendship are appreciated.

I'm indebted to Hunter Bass for his excellent attention to detail and probing questions. To Jennifer Cates and Stephanie Fellows, I am grateful for the encouragement when needed. Vaughan Davidson did a great job in creating another winning cover design.

My particular thanks go to Vicki Bass, who did the final editing, layout, design, and all of the other work no one does better.

Joanne, Tom, John, Sal, and Bill provided needed input. Andrew, Alex, Steve, Emily, Brandi, Lauren, Tami, Jenifer and all my friends at Applebee's kept me going on the days I needed a creative atmosphere.

Special thanks to all of my web clients and coaching clients for their comments, suggestions, and successes. They continue to be an inspiration to me!

Encouragement and Disclaimer

This book is designed to provide information on creating a more powerful business presence online. It is sold with the understanding that the publisher and author are not engaged in providing legal, accounting, or other professional services.

It is not the purpose of this book to reprint all of the information that is available to business decision-makers; but instead to complement, amplify, and supplement other sources of information. This book is most effective when you read all of the available material, learn as much as possible about building an effective online presence, and tailor the information to you and your business.

Having an effective online presence is not a quick job. With the changes in the Internet occurring so rapidly, it's a job that requires constant diligence and work. What works this year may be totally ineffective next year. So do not think you can do this once and be set for five years. That's not the way of the online world.

Every effort has been made to make this book as complete and accurate as possible. However, there may be errors, both typographical and in content. Therefore, this text should be used only as a general guide and not as the ultimate source of online information. Because online standards are changing constantly, information in this book will be updated on the accompanying website.

The purpose of this book is to educate and entertain. The author and Twin Towers Press shall have neither liability nor responsibility to any person or entity with respect to any losses or damages caused, or alleged to be have been caused, directly or indirectly, by the information contained in this book.

Table of Contents

The Internet is alive and well! Yet only one in three small businesses has a website. Of those, less than 10% are actually making any money from their site!

Obviously, you are one of the wise business people who recognizes the value of having a website and you are willing to work to make it better. Congratulations! This book was written for you.

Why this book

As I worked with many small business clients I saw a pattern. The business owner or manager knew little about their website, but a lot about the business. The web designer or technical guru knew a lot about the website, but little about the business.

The Online Business Mastery™ series is a direct result of that observation. No one is more qualified to make decisions for your business than you – the decision maker. So this book is written specifically for you. It will provide a series of ideas that can be implemented – many without any new technology.

What is Online Success?

There is no standard for defining online success yet. Instead, every business defines success according to the goals of the business and the purpose of their website. Regardless of the definition, there are four major reasons that businesses establish a website. None of the reasons stands alone; all of them are inter-related. However, sometimes one purpose stands out above the others. Which of the following best describes your purpose?

Increase revenue online

If you want to make money online, then you want to increase your online sales. For this you'll need a product or service you can sell online. You'll also need effective methods to raise the visibility of your website, as well as a way to provide extended service and support for clients and customers online.

Increase revenue offline

If you want to make money offline, then you can use your website to increase your visibility, which leads to more offline leads and hopefully more sales. Research has shown that up to 45% of consumers have purchased a product in a company's offline store after researching it on the company's website. The website becomes even more valuable when it is used to provide continued service and support after the sale.

Build your reputation and credibility

You may not be interested in increasing your income through use of your website. Instead, you may want to build your reputation and credibility by increasing your visibility. Publishing articles online, for example, is a quick way to enhance your credibility. Because publishing cycles online are much faster than traditional publishing, you have the potential to reach a wider audience faster than by using the print-based media. While activities designed to increase your visibility will not result directly in sales, they will provide more traffic coming to your site, and therefore more customer leads.

Support your customers, prospects and vendors

Naturally, providing support may also be combined with increased visibility and more online sales for the goals of a website. However, you may want to use your website primarily to support your customers, your prospects and your vendors before or after the sale. In this case, making a sale online may not be as important to you. Increasing your visibility may not be important.

But since you'll send your customers to your site before and after the sale, support is your major goal.

How this book is organized

Based on years of research, the Online Success System™ has taken the reasons you have a website and identified the three factors or dimensions of online success:

- Online Sales
- Visibility
- Service & Support

There is a section in this book that corresponds to each dimension.

The fourth section is dedicated to helping you, the business decision-maker, improve your expertise in the online business world.

At the back of the book you'll find a glossary to aid as you learn this new language of online success. The index is a quick way to find all the locations for a specific term or tactic. And the section on Where to Find more Information will lead you to online and offline resources.

How to use this book

This book is designed to be an idea and an action book. You should keep it with you as you move between appointments and when you travel. You can easily flip it open and read a tactic as your day progresses.

If you have a specific goal, look for the tactics in the appropriate section, then choose one or two tactics that are the easiest to implement. The tactics are arranged in each section roughly from easiest to most difficult, based on client experience, so the easier tactics are at the front of each section.

If you have multiple purposes for doing business online, you can start in any section of the book and choose a tactic at random. Regardless of your approach choose only two or three tactics to implement at a time.

If you're not sure where to start, just pick your favorite number and start reading. The important thing is to take action!

A word about Web-Enhanced™ Publications

This book is a Web-Enhanced™ book. It has a website that accompanies the book. This is critical to its long-term usefulness.

Without a website where we can post changes and updates, the information in this book would be outdated before it hit the bookstore shelves!

When you see the Web-Enhanced symbol at the bottom of a page, it means you will find more details about the tactic on the OnlineSuccessTactics website.

As the purchaser of this book you have access to a special portion of the web site. While the public can view a description of the book, only book owners can access the private portion of the site.

To get the password for the site send an email to updates@OnlineSuccessTactics.com. You will receive the current password by return email. We change the password frequently to ensure that only our members have access to the private area of the site. But once registered, you will receive the new password each time it is updated.

Now, let's start using the Online Success Tactics!

tactics \tac'tics\, n. Near term (very soon, usually within the next few weeks or months) actions taken to solve specific problems or accomplish specific goals.

Source: Investorwords.com

Tactics to Build Online Sales

The Online Sales dimension refers to the percentage of total sales derived from online sales and the source of that income. It does not reflect offline or non-Internet-based sales.

Online sales can come from a variety of sources. These include your products, your services, others' affiliate programs, an online catalog, or advertising. Generally the higher a company's online sales, the more likely they are to have multiple streams of online income.

The dimension of online sales is often confused with e-commerce. e-Commerce is the ability to sell from your website. But you do not necessarily need to have an e-commerce-enabled site in order to generate sales online; however, in most cases you will.

The tactics in this section include specific actions you can take, as well as ideas for product strategies you can follow to increase sales online.

Give Away Free Items

This may be free consulting, a free analysis, a free assessment, or a free report. Just give things away free. Most of the time, people who are online are looking for things that are free. In fact, the assumption is that everything on the Internet is free, so you want to provide some of that free information on your website as well.

Perhaps you offer a free report as an incentive for them to sign up for your email newsletter. You may offer a half hour of free consulting when they purchase a specific product. Know that even if you offer the half hour of free consulting, less than 10 percent of your clients are going to actually use that time. So don't be afraid to offer to give that time away. Not only will you have the opportunity to showcase your expertise if they do use it, but it generally will lead to additional sales and great word of mouth advertising from them if they are able to talk to you without charge.

You can offer a free analysis of some sort. For example, as an Internet expert, I offer a free three-point website analysis. Someone signs up and provides their content information in exchange for my going to their website and giving them three ideas to improve their website.

You can offer a free online assessment. Perhaps you are a marketing expert and want to give them feedback on their marketing strategies. You can offer an assessment for them to complete at your site in exchange for their contact information. You then send the results by email or provide them online.

Offer a Coupon

People love to save money. Coupons are a familiar method that do not require any explanation for most people.

Your coupon may be an email sent to all your regular subscribers offering them a free report if they type in the coupon's special number. Or it may be a special discount, a percentage or a dollar amount they'll receive by typing in that coupon number.

Your coupon needs to tie in to your shopping cart to be effective so that it is automatically subtracted at the time they place their order. If you don't have that capability, you can offer them an email coupon. After they have purchased the item, they can email you the coupon and you can write them a check, credit their account, or send them the free item they specified.

You can also offer a coupon to your un-connected customers. Mail a postcard with a coupon to your offline group. Tell them they can call you with their order to redeem their coupon.

Use Classified Ads

Classified ads are a good way to draw new business in the offline world. They are just as good in the online world.

Many people search through classified ads looking for new information and bargains. Use these classified ads to drive traffic to your web site.

There are numerous sites on the Internet that offer free classified ads. It is a way for them to draw visitors to their site, thus increasing their traffic and the ad rates they are able to charge. While you probably do not want to provide a site for free classified ads, you can take advantage of those that exist. To find them, search for "free classified ads" in your favorite search engine.

Classified ads are a great way to test your ad copy. You can create two ads offering the same product with different headlines. Direct each ad to a different page in your site. Then measure the results. After 2-3 weeks, choose the ad with the best response rate, then test that against a new ad. Continue this process until you can achieve predictable results from an ad, regardless of where you use it.

Classified ads also let you test different markets. Try an ad in a site that caters to one of your niche markets and the same ad at another site for another niche. Customize the ads for each niche as needed. You will draw traffic from a wider audience than if you just relied on the search engines.

Tactic #4

Offer Samples

Grocery stores caught on to this tactic years ago. In fact, many people ate their way through college weekends with free samples at the store! It works.

When you have a good product, the best way to have prospects agree with you is by giving them samples. How does this work in the online world? The same way it does in the offline world. However, if you're distributing an electronic product sample, it can be set up to be automatic. Thus, someone can request a "sample" by providing their name and email address and you can either email them the sample via an autoresponder (see Tactic #81) or you can send them to the page where the file can be downloaded.

Even if you're selling a physical product, you can provide a means for the prospect to sign up for the sample, providing their shipping information. You could offer the sample for the cost of shipping or for a reduced price. Or you could consider the shipping cost as the cost of marketing. Either way, the important thing is to get the sample in the hands of the customer.

This technique can be even more effective if you follow up with the prospect via email or a phone call.

Tactic #5

Write Benefits

When you are writing for the online environment, use benefits instead of features. Since you can't inquire as to the client's needs, you have to point out the benefits in the hope you will match your visitors' needs to the benefits you offer.

For example, "We have high-speed lines" is a feature. But "High-speed lines save you time and let you get home earlier" is a benefit.

To tell the difference between a feature and a benefit, ask the question "so what?"

We have high-speed lines.
So what?
That lets you get your work finished faster and lets you get home to your family.

We have a life-time guarantee.
So what?
You don't have to worry about anything going wrong at any time.

Tactic #6

Use Language Carefully

When you're writing for online consumption, you don't have the benefit of verbal feedback or facial clues to see if you are communicating effectively. Instead, you have to be more careful of the language you use.

Generally, humor does not work in an online environment, unless you add a <grin> or a <g> or a :-) . This will ensure your reader reads the humor as you intended. However, in more formal online writing, you do not usually use the abbreviations or emoticons (emotional icons such as the sideways happy face) that you do in informal correspondence with friends and clients who you know better. Therefore, using humor is always a gamble.

Likewise, be careful in the use of terms. For example, it is more attractive to mention the *investment* in your product or service, rather than the *price* of your service or product. Small wording changes can make a big difference.

It is a good practice to have someone outside of your company read your the web pages on your site. Since they bring a fresh perspective, they may find phrases and words that you overlooked.

Join Affiliate Programs

Affiliate programs provide a way for you to earn a commission by referring someone to another business website. For example, if you belong to the Amazon.com affiliate program, you receive a commission of 5-15% of the sale when someone goes from your site to Amazon to purchase a book, CD or other item.

Look for affiliate programs on merchandise that will be valuable to your clients. For example, if you work with home improvement businesses, you may want to join affiliate programs that offer tools, books on home improvement, plans for remodeling, and other related items.

Once you join, you post links leading to the other site, using your affiliate ID in the hyperlink. Then, when someone purchases an item from your link, you receive credit for the sale.

The beauty of affiliate programs is that you can offer items that are of value to your customers without having to warehouse the product, ship it, or process the sale. All you are doing is making a referral to another vendor – something you probably do on a regular basis already!

Tactic #8

Host a Virtual Trade Booth

Participate in an online trade show by renting a "virtual" trade booth. Some of these booths are tied to specific online or face-to-face conferences. Others are ongoing, such as those in an online mall. Often a virtual booth may be included in your exhibit fees if you are exhibiting live at a conference.

When you participate in the show, be sure to create an attractive offer that will get the booth visitors to sign up. For example, offer a free report if they sign up at your booth. Or offer a coupon for the live show if they sign up at your virtual booth. Either way, you will get their email so that you can follow up with them on a long-term basis.

Tactic #9

Form Joint Ventures

No site is an island. By recognizing this, you can tap into a much broader audience.

For example, if you already have a special report on customer service in the automotive field, you may want to enter into a joint venture with another site that specializes in contractors and do a special report on customer service in the construction field. They can market the report from their site because they have the visitors who are likely to purchase it. They then pay you the agreed-upon fee for that particular report.

Online joint ventures generally involve two experts who agree upon the need for a product and develop a plan for marketing it. It may be sold at both of their sites or just at one site. It may be sold at a new site or offered for sale via an affiliate program. Regardless of the means of distribution, it is important that the terms of payment between the venture "parties" are clear. Look for opportunities where you can take your core expertise and expand it to other areas by establishing joint ventures with other experts.

Tactic #10

Offer Gift Certificates

Gift certificates offer double advantages. You give your customers a gift by providing them with an easy way to honor and give to someone else (or keep for themselves!) In return, you get a new customer.

You can offer gift certificates online as a "product" that customers can purchase. When used, the gift certificate amount is taken off the total order of the merchandise in your online store. However, unless you have a strong following of customers who purchase regularly and you offer a wide variety of products, you are not likely to sell many gift certificates.

Instead, consider offering gift certificates as a reward to existing customers. For example, you can reward them with a $10 gift certificate when they refer five new customers to your site. Or you can offer them a certificate for a half-hour of consulting when they purchase one of your products.

You can also offer a gift certificate that your customers can pass on to someone else. When used, the gift certificate can trigger a thank you gift for your customer – making both your new customer and your existing customer happy!

Tactic #11

Offer an Affiliate Program

If you have several products or services that you want others to promote for you, set up an affiliate program. An affiliate program is a formal business practice. It requires a software program that provides each affiliate member with a unique referral ID. The software tracks sales for each ID and tells you how much to pay each affiliate at the end of the pay period.

In order to set up an affiliate program, you need to decide on the percentage of sales you will pay, how often you will pay commissions, and whether or not you have any other criteria for someone to become one of your affiliates.

You'll need software to track your affiliate program. And you'll need to commit to timely payment of your affiliates' earnings.

Finally, to be successful on a long-term basis, you need to offer good information and incentives for your affiliates. There are thousands of affiliate programs on the Internet. Why do they want to promote your products over someone else's? Provide that information and more! Give them banner ads, graphics, and text ads that are ready to use. Educate them on the ongoing benefits of your products. Offer contests and sales incentives. After all, these affiliates are your online sales force!

Do Things as a Series

In the discussion of building a brand (Tactic #53), the story of the variations on the Law & Order television shows illustrates the point of building a brand. However, it also illustrates how to build a series of products.

You should build a series with any group of articles or products that you produce. Don't just create one article; create one in a series. Creating a series helps maximize your marketing efforts by reinforcing the entire series each time you market one of the pieces. By creating a series, you create pieces that can be later combined into a whole.

For example, 10 individual articles can be combined into a special report. 100 articles can be combined into a book. 1,000 articles can be combined into a series of books! You get the idea!

Tactic #13

Think Layers

There are different layers of service, different layers of products, and different layers of client contact. Begin to think and plan what those layers are.

For example, you may answer general email information with an autoreponder (Tactic #81) within 24 hours and a customized response within 48 hours. That creates the first two layers of response. You may develop a way to flag all requests from existing customers, which you answer within 12 hours. This process creates the third layer of information service.

Do the same thing with your products, for example. You may have some products that are under $20 that are entry-level products. Then you have a group of products under $50, another under $100, then $250 and $500. Look at the different layers of products and make sure that you have a good spread within those different layers in order to provide the most attractive information to your client levels.

Repeat the process with your services. Offer some services priced at $200, others at $500 or $1000. Begin to think in layers of information, services, products, and client response times.

Tactic #14

Track Results

One of the big fears about doing business on the Internet is that you don't know what you're paying for. However, in reality, tracking the results of your activities online is easier than tracking traditional marketing activities.

When sending out an email with an offer in it, provide a link to a specific page. Then, given the number of emails you sent and the number of clicks on that page, versus the number of purchases from that page, you can track:

Response rate = clicks on page / emails sent
Conversion rate = purchases / clicks on page

If you send the same email to two different email lists, send each list to a separate page. You can clone a page easily so that the two pages are identical, with slightly different URLs.

Count the number of page views you receive on each page of your site. That way you know which pages are the most popular and can see what attracts visitors to your site. There are numerous page counters and traffic analysis pages on the Internet. Check first with your web hosting service to see what they include with your web site hosting fees.

Tactics to Build Online Visibility

The dimension of Visibility refers to the number and quality of site visitors, as well as the other ways in which a website is seen and promoted.

Visibility is the dimension that is most discussed when people talk about marketing online. They are actually referring to raising your visibility online. They are not talking about selling online.

Visibility is critical to online success because it is what brings visitors to your site. Without visitors you have no one to sell to or to support.

In order to be most effective in building your visibility, you need to define your target audience. While you may think your audience is "everyone," it is more likely they are a subset that you can define more precisely. Ask yourself, "If I were ordering mailing labels for my ideal customers, what description would I provide to the direct mail company?" This is your target audience. What is important to your visibility strategy is the amount of visibility you have with your target audience, not the Internet in general.

Traffic is another indicator of your website's visibility. By traffic, we are referring to the number of page views, not the number of "hits." A "hit" is a downloaded file. On a single web page you may have the page itself (one file) plus six graphics (six files). So when someone looks at that page, it is one page view or seven hits. You can see how meaningless "hits" are as an indicator of traffic, given the increasingly graphics-intense web pages created today. So page views are a better indicator of traffic than hits.

The tactics in this section include specific actions you can take to improve your visibility online. While some of the tactics are completed offline, they will lead to your online success. And that, of course, takes you one step closer to overall business success!

Tactic #15

Collect Email Addresses

Email addresses are the currency for online business. With an email address you can contact a prospect or customer without any cost to you. You can provide quality followup to a sales or information presentation. You can offer new products as they are announced. You can seek input for ideas you have that will benefit the addressee. In short, you can stay in touch.

Start now to organize email addresses you already have on hand. Put these into a database so that you can access them easily. You'll be using these email addresses in many of the other tactics offered in this book.

Seek Email Addresses

It's not enough to organize the email addresses you already have. You must start to actively seek email addresses.

Put a signup form on every page of your website. Just having a single page with a form won't work. Online, you can never tell where a visitor will enter your site or where they will exit. So it needs to be on every page.

On the form, request their email address. You don't need their name, address or telephone number. You can get that information later when they become a customer. For now, all you need is their email address. Once they get to know you, they will be more likely to share their other information with you.

Check that every business card you receive has an email address on it. If not, ask for it.

When you give a presentation, offer a free report or a subscription to your email newsletter if they give you their business card with their email address.

If you have a substantial client base for whom you don't have email addresses, send out a request for their email addresses. Offer something in return, like a free report. Then, either have them send a postcard with their update or ask them to go online and complete the form.

It's always easier to get something in exchange for something. Sometimes, your email newsletter is not as high a perceived value as a free report. So create an offer that will make it easier for them to sign up.

Tactic #17

Use a Signature File

A signature file is a block of text that you append to the end of every email. While it generally contains your name, your email address, your website, your phone and fax and sometimes your address, you may offer only that information that you want the general public to see. Your signature file may also contain an advertising message.

A signature file is one of the few ways you can advertise online without being accused of sending "spam" (unsolicited email). By adding your one or two-line ad to your signature file, it's considered a part of who you are.

To set up a signature file, look in the help menu of your email program. Then follow the directions given there.

Here is my typical signature file:

Jeanette S. Cates, PhD
Technology Implementation Expert
http://www.TechTamers.com
Author of Online Success Tactics
http://www.OnlineSuccessTactics.com

Tactic #18

Change Your Signature File Often

You can have more than one signature file. So use different versions for different purposes.

You can have one signature file that you attach to email to prospective customers.

Create another signature file for existing clients, promoting your newest product.

Have another signature file that gives the date of your upcoming public appearances.

And yet another can provide all of your contact details, so you don't have to type all of that information when you request something be sent to you.

Tactic #19

Ask for Information

There is nothing new under the sun. You've heard that saying. Nowhere is that more true than on the Internet. Everything you want to do has been done already. All you need to do is find out who has done it and where they have done it. Then you can ask questions.

If you see a website technique you like, email the webmaster and ask how they did it. If it's not immediately obvious how you can do it on your site, ask how much it would cost to have them do it for you.

If you see an article you would like to have on your site, email the author and ask permission to reprint the article, offering to give the proper credit and a link back to their site.

If you see a site where you think your site would be a good additional resource, email the site owner and ask to trade links.

Ask for Referrals

In his email newsletter, technology speaker and internet marketing guru Tom Antion (Antion.com) asks for referrals. He books several speeches every year from referrals from his readers. It pays to ask for referrals!

Ask your newsletter readers to forward a copy of your newsletter to anyone else who might be interested.

Ask your website visitors to use a refer-a-friend form to invite their friends to visit your site.

Offer an email-a-friend form so that visitors to your site can send the contents of one of your web pages to someone else. Point out that this is the electronic equivalent of the yellow sticky on the copy of the article that you used to "snail mail" (via the postal service) to your clients. For more about this idea, see Tactic #72.

Offer a Referral Fee

Professional speaker and Internet marketing expert Robert Middleton (ActionPlan.com) offers a free product to visitors who refer three of their friends to his site.

If you ask people to refer you and your website, offer a referral fee. Perhaps you offer them a discount coupon for your products when they refer 5 people to your site. Or if they refer 10 people to sign up for your email newsletter, they get a free copy of one of your special reports.

There is no stronger link to ongoing business than referral from a satisfied customer. Be willing to pay for it!

Give Advice – Free and Unsolicited

There is often the perception in business that everything you do must yield a profit. This is not true – especially when it comes to sharing advice.

As an Internet expert, I spend a lot of time online. I often find broken links, broken graphics, and poor website navigation. While I could ignore these items and go on about my surfing, I prefer to share the information with the site owner. Not once has anyone ever said it was none of my business. In fact, many have written to thank me.

What advice can you offer? You don't need to seek opportunities to give advice. But don't shy away from opportunities when you find them. Offer advice in the spirit of a helping hand. Include why you are qualified to offer this advice. Sometimes it's because you're an expert; sometimes because you're a prospect; other times just because you care and don't want to see an error that might embarrass the website owner.

Include any pertinent information that will make it easier for the website owner to contact you. And be sure to include your signature file! You never know when that person will need the product or service you have to offer.

Wear Your URL

Just as you create specialty items with your URL (see Tactic #45), you also want to create clothing items and other ways that you can wear your URL. When you dress in casual clothes, why not advertise your services with an embroidered polo shirt with your URL and name on it? You would be amazed at the attention and questions you can get just walking around the mall with your logo on your shirt or hat.

Wear a bumper sticker on your car that highlights your expertise and URL. Put a window sticker on your car with your URL in it. Have all of your family members put the window sticker on their cars.

Embroider a bag that you carry on planes and trips with your URL and business name on it.

Offer the logo items to your top 25 list as a gift for them. They will be glad to advertise your business as they wander the mall or travel on a plane.

Tactic #24

Contact Your Top 25 Monthly

One of the most effective marketing techniques you can use is to identify the top 25 influencers who generate leads or business for you and your website. These influencers may be key people who recommend you for business or who do the hiring, or they may be people who maintain a broad network and refer you to others for business. Your top 25 may include people you *want* to do business with. In any case, 25 is a manageable number.

By staying in touch with your top 25 on a regular basis, you are able to keep your name and information uppermost in their consciousness. These people are generally already impressed with you and therefore, are receptive to receiving information from you.

Decide how you will contact them each month. It could be via phone, email, or with an article you send to them. You might send them a postcard as you travel. You could send a small gift that is meaningful only to them. Make it something that lets them know you are thinking of them, specifically, as an individual.

Offer Specialty Items

Specialty items are the small give-away items with your logo and message on them. They can range from t-shirts to bumper stickers to coffee mugs to key chains.

Offer specialty items that have your website URL as well as your logo and your business name on them. These items could be magnets, stress balls, or anything at all that seems appropriate for your business.

The easiest items to use are pens with all your information on them. Pens are good give-aways to leave behind. You can "forget" a pen at the bank, at the grocery store or at your local restaurant. Someone else will come along and pick it up!

Your specialty items should provide something that is memorable for your prospects or customers. It could be a tag line or a quote that you use regularly. It could be an item that is useful, such as a calendar or memo pad. David Zach (DavidZach.com), to advertise his book of *Zachronyms*, provided post-it note pads with different cartoons from the book. You can use anything that provides a good reason for your prospects and customers to keep that specialty item around.

Tactic #26

Use Your Promotional Literature

All of the literature that you use for marketing or any type of promotion should always have your website URL on it. People are more likely to visit your website than they are to call you to ask for additional information.

If you have any type of direct mail campaign, you definitely want to have information about your website. This should include where they can go to get additional information about your business, your areas of expertise, your products and services, and your capabilities. The information on your website could be beyond what they typically find on the literature itself or it may be a printable copy of the literature that they can download.

You want to ensure that your website URL is on every marketing piece. If you aren't prepared to reprint your literature, you can always print stickers with your website on them. Add them and say, "Just announced."

Use the URL stickers on your envelopes when you are sending out information. That helps to bring your website to the top of mind for everyone who sees your literature and your message.

Tactic #27

Use Email Effectively

Email is your primary communication tool online. Not only do you use it to maintain contact with your existing clients, but you also use it to market to new prospects. Since you spend so much of your time with email online, it is worth the effort to learn to use it appropriately.

To learn more about effective email, you can attend a class at your local community school, take an online course, or read a book.

Sell with Your Business Card

Too often business cards look like they have been stamped from the same mold. Why not use your business card to test your marketing?

With the advent of quality color printing you can print small quantities of your business cards in your office. Produce 10 cards of one design and 10 of another, then hand them out at a networking event. You can judge the effectiveness of one design over another by the number of follow up responses you receive from each of the two designs.

What do you put on the different designs? Change the tagline. Change your title. Change the design. You can put the picture of one of your products on a card. You can even put a picture of your website on your business card! Whatever attracts attention and makes your card memorable is what you want to use.

Naturally, your business card should always include your email address and your site's URL.

Provide a Tips Sheet

Everyone likes tip sheets. The top ten ways to do a particular process. The top five ways to generate more business. Anytime you can put something into a list or a tips sheet, you want to offer that to your clients, either through a free autoresponder (Tactic #81), on your website, or even as a paid item.

Think in terms of top 10, top 25, top 100 tips sheets. As you are creating ideas, try to put those in a tips sheet so that you have that much more content that you can offer. You may offer a tips sheet of the month on a subscription basis, free of charge or even for a small charge.

Many newspapers and other print publications are looking for tips sheets. This is a wonderful way to get your information published in a print publication.

Newsletter editors are always looking for tips sheets they can include as filler in their company newsletter or email newsletter. Offer your tips sheet to a wide audience and they will pay off for you in the long run.

Tips sheets evolve, so many tips sheets become booklets, compilations, or even books.

Tactic #30

Send a Postcard

Many of your potential web visitors are not yet online, or if they are, they are only using email. One of the best ways you can contact them about your website is to send them a web card. That is a postcard that has a picture of your website on it and the message on the back includes reasons they may want to visit your website. If you offer a tips sheet or a special report, highlight it on the back of the postcard so recipients know they can come to your website in order to pick up their free tips sheet.

Send out the same postcard to the same list twice within two weeks. That generally will increase your response rate by 5-10%.

If you offer a special at your website, send a postcard to your offline visitors to let them know about your website special. If you think that many of them do not have access to the Internet, you can offer that same online special via postcard with a telephone number for them to call. You can use a fax on demand number to distribute the order blank or a special report.

Another good way to build traffic with postcards is to offer postcards online. This is particularly effective if you have artistic ability or have a group of visuals that you use in your presentations that others would like to share with their friends. These make great online postcards.

Do Book Reports

No, these are not the book reports you had to do in school. These are the book reports that will be useful to your website visitors.

None of us have enough time to read everything we want to read. So relying on someone else's summary of the book is often the best we can do. Especially if it's someone we consider an expert and whose opinion we value! That makes the book report doubly valuable to us.

When doing a book report you can provide a summary of the book, a list of your favorite points or quotes, or perhaps relate a topic from the book to a concept within your field of expertise. Regardless of the format, it will be valuable to your readers. If you recommend the book, say so, and specify the type of reader who would most benefit from or enjoy the book.

When you recommend a book, you can provide an added service by linking your web site visitors to an online bookstore that sells the book. If you do this, be sure to set up an affiliate program with the online bookstore so that you can reap a small monetary reward from your recommendation.

Follow up with Technology

You are often given the opportunity to present your service or product in a live face-to-face setting, in an office, a meeting or at a conference. Your message will have a greater impact if you follow up this presentation with online technology.

To do this, prior to the presentation, compose a series of email messages. The first should be a "thank you for attending" message. The following six to twelve messages should be the main concepts that you stressed in your presentation. Send one of these email messages each week for the next six to twelve weeks.

Your recipients will have one of three reactions to the information:
"I knew that! I'm so smart."
"Gee, I'm glad she reminded me of that. I had forgotten the specifics."
"Wow! Brand new information."
Regardless of the reaction, it's a win-win reaction.

In addition to the content you send, you can direct the recipient to specific products or pages on your web site that provide additional information on that topic.

You can send these email follow up messages either through your email program or through a sequential autoresponder. Either way, your prospects will see your name and contact information over a three-month period. Plus you'll have multiple opportunities to offer them products, information, and services.

Tactic #33

Prepare an Online Marketing Plan

Just as you prepare a marketing plan for your business, you should have an online marketing plan for your business. You may combine the two. However, because the strategies and tactics are often different, many businesses prepare them separately.

One of the easiest ways to prepare an online marketing plan is to list the four to six goals you have for your online business this year. Then beneath each goal, list the primary activities you will do to accomplish those goals. Be sure to specify the dates when the activities will be completed and how you will measure the results.

When you have completed the plan, put all of the activities on the calendar so that you will know when to begin each activity. A good place to start your online marketing plan would be with the tactics outlined in this book. If you implemented each of these over the coming year, where would your online business be in 365 days?

Use an Email Address @ Your Website

Many people start using the Internet with America Online (AOL.com). Thousands of people have signed up for a free email account with Hotmail (Hotmail.com). But when it comes to business, your email address should reflect your own website.

By using an email address at your domain (your website address), it reinforces your brand. It automatically identifies you as "from" that domain. While many people will discard email from AOL or Hotmail, they will be more likely to respect your email when they recognize your domain name.

You don't have to give up your AOL or Hotmail account. Instead, you can forward your email address at your domain to your other account. That way you can pick up your email through AOL or Hotmail, even when you're traveling. Ask you Web Presence Provider (WPP) who hosts your website how to forward your domain email to your AOL or Hotmail account.

When you reply to email, use your domain email address as the "reply to" address. This will ensure that your domain email address shows in the "to" field when someone replies to your email. Use the help menu in your email program to learn how to set up the "reply to" address.

Hang Out with Your Prospects

There are websites which your ideal prospects frequent, looking for information. These sites may be associations, information sites, new sites, or other sites that offer the type of atmosphere your prospects seek. Be sure you're where they can find you.

Offer your articles to these frequently visited sites.

If they offer online discussions, read the questions and contribute answers regularly. While it is not appropriate for you to "advertise" on these discussions, it is okay to add a 4 to 6 line signature file to your email postings, providing information about your business.

Subscribe to the newsletters from these sites. Again, if they offer a forum for people to ask questions, be one of the first to offer advice. If the newsletter editor writes an article with which you agree or disagree, email your comments. Most newsletters need content, so your comments are often posted in the next issue. Remember that newsletters are an ideal target for your articles as well!

Join and Lurk in Discussion Lists

Discussion lists are a way to carry on a conversation online. Because all of the participants do not have to be online at the same time, it fits into business lives easily. A good discussion list has a series of messages that open new topics, then replies to the topics – and replies to the replies! All of the participants add to the discussion as they view the messages online.

Look for the discussion lists where your target audience talks about issues. Join those lists. "Lurk," or just read the postings for a week or two until you know the type of postings that are sent, the format, and the types of discussions going on in that particular list.

Once you feel comfortable with the type of information shared on the list, you can begin to post your answers and your perspective on the various topics. Be sure to include an appropriate signature file on each posting. This is a quiet way of advertising that is perfectly acceptable on a discussion list. It's a way for you to highlight your expertise in your content, as well as your signature file.

Be Sure Associations Have Your URL

If you work within one industry, you want to be sure all of the relevant trade associations link to your URL. In some cases, you may need to pay for this listing. In other cases, you may need to register as a resource in that content area. In still other cases, you may want to publish an article in the trade magazine, either online or offline.

In all cases, you want to be sure your target audience is seeing a link to your URL coming from their association. This not only lends credibility to you, but it also drives traffic to you.

Advertise at Expert Sites

There are a number of expert sites online that deal with different topics. Most of them have areas with a variety of topics. If you are an expert in publicity or media, for example, you may want to register as an expert at experts.com in the area dedicated to media. When someone asks the question in that area, the request is sent out to all the experts registered there. You draft your response to the person asking the question.

Many times responding to these questions can lead to additional contracts for you, to speaking engagements, or to a nice affiliation with someone who can recommend you to others.

In your responses on these expert sites, be generous with your information and always include your signature file with whichever product or service you want to highlight for that prospective customer. Prospects assume that if you provide lots of quality information for free that there is even more available for an additional fee. Never be afraid to share your expertise. It will only help build your credibility.

List on Media Directories

Media exposure is a great way to build the visibility of your business, both online and offline. In some cases you can get to know the reporters in your area in order to be featured in newspaper articles. However, getting media coverage on a national basis may be more difficult.

Reporters and magazine writers often rely upon standard references to find the experts that they interview. So if you want to be interviewed by the national media, you need to appear on sites such as The Yearbook of Experts (Yearbook.com) or the Radio-TV Interview Report (rtir.com). Depending on how crowded your field of expertise is, you may need to pay for a larger ad in order to be noticed within these resources. However, it is definitely worth your while to generate traffic from these media directories, then measure the results from your ad.

Comment on Current Events

Current events provide another way to show your expertise. When you have a website, you have the ear of those who visit your site, as well as those who subscribe to your ezine.

So when an event occurs that impacts your business area, comment on it. Give the source of the original information and perhaps quote some of it. Then give your point of view, pro or con.

A current event can trigger a good article for your website or ezine (see Tactic #52). Or you can phrase the current event as a question for your Ask the Expert column (see Tactic #69). Regardless of the format you choose, show that you keep up with the news with this tactic.

Write Articles

As an expert, you should be writing articles about your areas of expertise. These articles are pieces of information that are helpful to your end user. If you don't consider yourself a writer, hire someone to ghost write your articles, based on interviews with you.

Every article should include your contact information in a short bio paragraph at the end of the article and, ideally, an email address where they can write for more information about that topic (refer to the autoresponder tactic in Tactic #81).

You need to publish these articles on your website and in your email newsletter in order to showcase your expertise for your own website visitors and subscribers. But you also want to include a paragraph below each article on your website giving permission for reprint of that article on any other website or in any other email newsletter as long as the bio information is included, in its entirety, as written, along with a live link back to your site.

By doing this, you set yourself up as a publisher of content that others can use to reach prospects. Even if some of your prospects are reading their newsletter, as they begin to see your name "everywhere" they'll recognize what a widely known expert you are.

Offer Articles to Other Sites

The articles you write are valuable not only to your site visitors, but to others as well. By having your articles published on other sites, you provide more ways for people to see your information and want to visit your site. Each link back to your site adds to your link popularity, thus raising your visibility in some of the search engines. So it benefits you, as well as the readers, to have your articles on a variety of sites across the Internet.

One way to offer free articles for reprint is to create a page of links to your articles. Then register that page on the search engines with the key phrases of "free articles" and "free reprints".

Another way is to register your articles on some of the article sharing sites. One such site is EzineArticles.com, where authors can offer their articles. Then website owners and ezine publishers who are looking for content can request articles. To find other article exchange sites, search for "free articles" in a search engine.

In addition to offering these articles on your website, you can also send an email to the editor of a newsletter in which you would like to be published, offering them articles and giving them the URL where they can find multiple articles from you.

Regardless of your area of expertise, you need to be writing and sharing articles!

Contact Media Regularly

Reporters and writers are constantly on deadline, needing more information daily. You can be a valuable resource to them. But you need to let them know how you can help.

Gather email addresses for writers whose work you admire. Nowadays bylines for articles contain an email address for the writer. You can also check the company directory for most publications to get email addresses.

When you see an article you like or one that you disagree with, send an email message to the author. Writing can be a lonely business, with little feedback on what you do. So most writers are very glad to hear from you.

Get to know the reporters you want to work with. When possible, meet with them face-to-face. Since everyone has a preferred communication mode (phone, fax, or email), learn what each person prefers and contact them in that way.

When you have a story idea, send it to the appropriate contact.

When there is an event where you could contribute as an expert, contact the appropriate writer and offer your ideas and expertise. When you can provide background information on the event, send it to them via their preferred communication mode.

Tactic #44

Send News Releases and Announcements

News releases are an important part of your visibility tactics. They are the accepted method for providing information to the media outlets.

There are several announcement services that will allow you to send out announcements to the press or to selected members of the press. Or you can send out your own news announcements to those press contacts with whom you have created a personal relationship.

Format your news releases exactly as you would a print-based press release. When sending it via email, include the news release information in the body of the email. Your contacts are more likely to read a news release in the body of an email than take the time to double-click to get to an attachment.

Remember to post your news releases on your website.

Publish Articles that Others Write

You don't have to create all of the content for your website or your
email newsletter. Instead, you can use content from others. Generally, in exchange for this content, you will include their bio paragraph along with a link to their website.

Using articles from other experts begins to give you leverage in
terms of serving your area of expertise and serving your clients
with expertise from a broad range. If you are the only publisher of
information on your website, your visitors are likely to think that
you are self-serving. However, if you are making an honest effort
to point them to the best resources on particular topics, regardless
of source, they are much more likely to see you as a source of
information rather than the creator of a limited amount of information. You are more likely to be viewed as the expert.

You can get these content articles from other websites or from
ezine registration sites such as EzineArticles.com, where people
have purposely put their articles to be used by others in exchange
for that short paragraph and tie back to their website.

When using content from another site, be sure you have permission
to do so. If in doubt, request permission via email to verify any
requirements the copyright holder has for the publication of their
content.

Naturally, it's always courteous to send a thank-you email to the
author of an article, telling them you have posted their content and
giving them the URL.

Trade Links

One of the growing areas of popularity is linking between sites with related information. Not only do your prospects and clients appreciate that, but the search engines are beginning to lend credibility to that as well. So given two sites of equal content, the site that has more links leading to it will rank higher in the search engine results than the one without links to it.

It is to your benefit to have more sites that are linking to your site for content. Likewise, it is to your benefit and to your clients' and visitors' benefits that there are additional links leading from your site back to other good resources on that particular topic.

Plan a link trading strategy. First, design a page where your traded links will appear. Next, compose what you would like other sites to say about your site. If you have a logo that you want them to use in addition to the verbage, give them the URL.

Send an email to another website owner where you would like a link to your site to appear and offer to trade links. Provide the verbage you would like as well as the logo you want included on the link. Ask them for the same information in exchange. Tell them where their link will appear.

Link trading is a relatively slow process but, in the long run, is extremely effective. It is a wonderful way for you to get additional traffic as well as provide better information for your visitors.

Put Your Picture on Articles

People identify with you more as a person when they are able to see you. Include a picture with every article you write, particularly on your website. Get a variety of poses so they don't see the same head shot every time.

If you are publishing in a professional field, you will probably restrict your photos to more formal head shots. However, you can include pictures of you and other people mentioned in the article, if you have the photographs and permission to print them.

If you have a digital camera, you might take a photograph that relates specifically to the article. One way to customize the photo is to add a caption balloon coming from your head with a caption specific to that article. Or, if it is something that lends itself to costume, you could wear a different costume for each article that ties back to that topic.

Look for ways to be creative with your photos, but as often as practical, include a picture of yourself on the articles that you write so people will automatically relate to you more closely.

Prepare Special Reports

Special reports are an in-depth study of a specific topic. They are "an inch-wide and a mile deep" (PublicityHound.com).

Special reports are an ideal way for you to display your expertise in depth on a specific topic. They are a good information product to be sold online and a good way to start with information publishing. You can offer a special report as an incentive for someone who signs up to receive your ezine. Or you can offer a special report as something that someone could get as a bonus for signing up for seminars.

To prepare a special report, take one of your general topics and outline the 25 topics that you would cover in a day-long seminar. Take each one of those topics and make a special report on it.

Special reports can be anywhere from 8–50 pages long depending on the topic and your writing style, as well as the number of illustrations you might include in them.

Ask for Awards

When you see an "award-winning" site, are you impressed? Probably. Most people are. After all, if your site is winning awards, then it must be good.

So how do you get to be an award-winning site? You ask for it! There are numerous websites that offer awards for your site. While some of these judge your website against a set criteria or have a formal panel of judges, many of these sites provide awards in order to build their traffic. When you put their award on your site, you provide a link back to them and they automatically get more traffic!

To find awards, do a search in your favorite search engine.

Look for awards on other sites and find out where they came from. If you need to, send an email to the webmaster and ask them about the award and the application process. Online, you need to blow your own horn!

Remember when you win an award, you need to publish a news release about it. Send it to your local press and all of your media contacts, particularly in your industry.

Include the award logo and link back to the awards site on your front page, then link the award to your online press release.

Have a Contest

One of the best ways to increase the traffic to your site is a contest. People love to get something free. This is especially true online.

You can have a contest that offers a large prize such as a cruise. Or you can offer a free ebook to every 100th visitor. Whatever you offer as a prize, the key is good advertising.

Advertise your contest with free online classified ads.

Register the contest page in each of the major search engines, emphasizing the word "free".

Advertise your contest in your ezine.

Provide a refer-a-friend form where people register for the contest. That will make it easy for them to send the contest information to their friends. In fact, why not offer a contest for the person who makes the most referrals!

Have One or More Websites

While you can do business online without a website, it is expected that you have a website if you are a legitimate business. Often people will check your website before they call your business or come in to look around.

Having more than one website can be a good tactic. With more than one website, you can name websites that are equivalent to the keywords your prospects will be looking for when they search for you. For example, if you are an automotive repair shop, you may want to have

carengines.com
batteries.com
transmissionrepairs.com, etc.

While many of those URLs are already taken, you can use some creativity in keywords for new website names. For example, where-to-repair-my-car.com will likely show at the top of the list for that specific question, since it *is* the question.

If you have multiple domains, you can either have all of them point to one place (a time-saver for site maintenance) or have each of your sites point to each of the others. This second technique will help to build traffic at all of your sites and will help raise your rankings in some of the search engines. This is because several of the search engines rank sites on the basis of "link popularity." Therefore, the more links you have coming to your site and going from your site, the higher you will rank in the search engines results.

Publish an Ezine

An ezine (an electronic magazine) is critical to your success online. It lets you stay in touch with your customers, prospects, and vendors. Your ezine is your link to your site visitors. Through the ezine they get to know you, how you think, and what you value. They learn about products and services that you recommend. In short, they build a level of trust in you.

People coming to your web site usually don't know you personally. Instead, they have to rely on clues to decide if you're a legitimate business. They look at your web site and its professional appearance. They look to see if your address and phone number are listed. They check out the types of information you provide. They look at the resources you offer. Beyond that, they have no way to get to know you better – except through your ezine.

Before someone is willing to take out their wallet and spend money on your site or in your store, they need to trust you. And this trust goes beyond having a secure connection on your shopping cart. It involves their knowing and trusting you and your company – online as well as offline.

Tactic #53

Develop a Brand

A brand is a clearly identifiable image that immediately brings you and your company to mind. A brand can be specified by an image (a logo, such as the one AT&T spent millions of dollars to create), a tagline (Cotton - the fabric of our lives) or even a font (CocaCola is immediately identifiable by the script used).

Your business probably already has the start of a brand. Carry through that same brand online. Use your business colors in your website. Use your logo. Use your tagline.

When you expand, do so in a logical manner. The television series Law and Order did just that. From their initial show, they added a series on Special Victims Unit, then on Criminal Intent. Each program carries the Law & Order logo, with a slight variation. Each program's musical theme is a variation of the original. They have a brand.

When you establish a brand, you should take the time and make the investment of protecting your brand. This may be the trademark of your logo or the patent of a process. In either case, your brand is worth the investment.

What brand do you have? Does your online brand match your offline brand? Does your brand represent the image you want to convey?

Offer a Press Room

Members of the media can be some of your best friends in publicizing your website. Most writers and reporters have one deadline after another to meet, so they are always looking for good stories, breaking news, and "filler" they can use.

You can help by providing a section on your website specifically for the media. Here are some of the things you might want to include in your media section:

- News releases on your company and activities
- Photos of you and your company, ready for publication
- Background information on your company
- Quotes from you, ready for reprint
- Links to articles on topics of expertise
- Tips that newsletter editors can use without contacting you

By providing these items in your media section, reporters and writers will soon learn that they can find good information at your site. Sometimes, when they cannot reach you for a quote, they can use a quote from your site. If a newsletter editor needs an article or a tip to fill a column, they will use one of yours. Your materials will be published and quoted everywhere!

Start an Awards Program

If your area of expertise lends itself to having awards, then you'll want to start your own awards program. You want to offer this for other websites so people can come and register at your site or nominate their website for one of your awards. If your business, for example, specializes in customer service training, you can have a program for the top 100 customer service websites.

Along with the award, you can also create a special logo that the winning site can include on their website. That logo, of course, will lead back to your website where people can get information about the award – and your business. This helps to advertise your business and also adds credibility to other people's businesses. So it becomes a mutually beneficial program by bringing them prestige while they identify themselves to you as prospects for alliances and business.

Let people nominate themselves for the award. If you prefer, they can nominate other sites, bringing a letter of thanks to the nominator and a congratulations to the nominee. That way it's a win-win-win solution.

Form Online Marketing Groups

If you are selling to a specific target audience, it makes sense to join forces with others who sell to the same market. For example, if you are a professional organizer for small businesses, you may want to team with an accounting firm who specializes in working with small businesses.

You can offer links to the accounting firm from your site and they can do the same for you. When they mail an advertising piece, you can "piggyback" on their mailing, whether it's online or offline. You can offer joint discounts for clients who purchase a package involving both of you. Each of you can include tips in the other's ezine.

Always be on the lookout for businesses which are interested in the same target market you are. Then look for ways you can form an online marketing group. The larger the group, the less expense to each member and the broader the reach of the group.

Tactic #57

Reformat and Repurpose

When you have information, you can present it in a variety of ways. For example, you can have a tip of the day or you can have a tip of the week. You can provide 30 tips in a booklet format. Or you could have a year-long course with one tip per day. Each of these different formats uses the same information but in different ways.

You can do the same with repurposing your information. For example, you can use an article as part of your email newsletter, then post it on your web site as a separate article. You can send that article to other online publishers or send it to print magazine publishers. You can write an article on how to market to your target market, then rewrite it to show how the same principles are applicable to a different target market.

When you think of information, ask yourself how can I reformat this information? What others ways can I use it?

Tactics to Build Online Support

The dimension of Support refers to the internal and external depth of service and support provided for your online presence.

Service and support deal with how you relate to the major groups of visitors to your site. They are your existing customers, your prospects, and your vendors.

For each of these groups, you'll want to look at how you respond to them. For example, when you receive an email from a customer, do you respond more quickly than if you receive an email from a prospect or a vendor? Or do you respond to members of all three groups in the same manner?

Do you seek input – ideas and suggestions – from each of the three groups? Are they included in surveys and focus groups on what they would find most helpful at your website or in other parts of your business?

Do you customize any content on your website for members of each group? Many companies, for example, provide FAQs to answer questions for each group.

The key is relationships. While you attract people to your web site through visibility tactics, you keep them there through good service and support.

The tactics in this section include specific actions you can take to improve your online service and support – and thereby your online relationships.

Tactic #58

Maintain a Contact Database

The value of your business can often be equated with the value of your list. Nowhere is this more true than with your business online.

At a minimum your database needs to contain your contact's name and email address. Most people are willing to give this information in exchange for a subscription or free product. However, if you ask for more information, you may meet resistance. After all, if you're going to send them an email, do you really need their street address? They probably don't think so.

On the other hand, they may be willing to give you their zip code. This is helpful for several purposes. First, if you offer live seminars or events, having the zip code helps you market upcoming events. If you sell a higher-priced product or service, a zip code analysis can help you identify your most likely targets by determining average income in a zip code.

Put Contact Information on Each Page

You never know which page will attract a visitor. Coming from a search engine, they may enter your site on one of the back pages and never see your front page. Likewise, they may print and keep one of those back pages and not print your Contact page.

To be safe and to provide better information to your visitors, include full contact information on every page of your site. Incorporate it into your design so that it is viewable everywhere they go in your site.

Use Their Name

To each person, their name is the sweetest word in the language. Therefore, it is important to use the recipient's name as often as possible, especially in email.

You can personalize email manually or with a mail merge program. Many of the contact managers and the bulk email programs have this capability built in.

Personalized email is particularly effective in the subject line. Everyone likes to see their name and they're more likely to open the email if their name is the first thing they see on the subject line.

It's also very effective to use their name in the body of the email, right before you make an important point. This "wakes them up" when they see their name and they are more likely to pay attention to the information that follows.

Follow the Platinum Rule

Growing up your mother probably reminded you of the Golden Rule "Do unto others as you would have them do unto you." Today that has been revised to the Platinum Rule (PlatinumRule.com): "Do unto others as they would like done unto them!" Treat others as they want to be treated.

This is a combination of tactics in the online world. It means putting a subject line on your email messages so that the readers can determine whether or not they need to open it immediately. It means not sending a message marked "urgent" unless it is. It means making your online purchasing process easy to use and easy to buy. It means providing the type of information your customers want to see on a web site.

What else can you think of that would make an Internet traveler's life easier? How can you apply that to your site for your customers? Remember, what works for you may not be the best solution for your visitor. Instead, spend time and energy understanding what they need and want.

Tactic #62

Say Thank You

After appearing on a television show, a professional speaker sent a thank you note to the producer, thanking him for his time and helpfulness on the set. The producer called to thank her for sending the note. Surprised, she said "I would imagine in your position you receive thank you's all the time." The producer replied "This is the first thank you note I've gotten in 15 years."

This is true in the online world as well. When you see an order come across your email, you know the customer has received their confirmation email as well. But if you'll take a minute to write a personal thank you email, you'll be amazed at the response. Suddenly they feel special and have a real connection with you, the person, rather than just with your shopping cart.

Postcard guru Alex Mandossian (MarketingWithPostcards.com) takes this one step further. Alex usually picks up the phone and thanks the customer personally. You can imagine their surprise and delight in receiving a phone call from the author himself!

Use the same technique when someone subscribes to your newsletter. Sure, they will get an automatic response from the email engine, but how much more special to get a thank-you directly from you! It's the start of many good friendships.

Seek Customer Input

Your customers are your biggest cheering squad. They have already purchased your service or product and are rooting for your success.

One of the highest compliments you can pay your customers is to ask for their help and input. They want to see you succeed and they love being asked their opinion. So provide email or web site surveys. Post new ideas and designs, then ask for their opinion.

John Kremer (Bookmarket.com) posted two possible cover designs for the new edition of his *1001 Ways to Market your Book*. He was surprised that one cover was the choice of his web visitors – by a margin of 9 to 1! Guess which cover he used for the book?

If you're considering writing a special report, but are uncertain which topic to cover first, send an email and ask which report your customers would purchase first. You can do the same to "test" potential titles for an article or book.

Remember, as with all business transactions, to say 'thank you.'

Tactic #64

Respond Quickly

You should respond quickly not only to your email but to any discussion groups or newsletters you receive.

As you are reading a discussion or a newsletter, respond immediately to it. Most editors are on a tight deadline to get the next issue out. Your prompt response to a question will provide them the content they need to get out the next issue. If you delay your response until you "have time" or until its "perfect," your response will probably not make it into the next issue or any future issues once that question has been dropped.

The ability to respond quickly pays off in many ways. In one instance, for example, I landed two columns that pay me a monthly fee because of my quick response to a request for experts in these specific fields. In another instance, I was invited to be a columnist based on the quality of content I included in my response to a question coming through an email newsletter. Both of these opportunities have yielded a lot of additional opportunities to me, but they all would have been missed had I delayed my response to make it perfect.

Involve Your Staff

If you are lucky enough to have staff to help with your business, involve them early and often in your online business.

For example, in the web design division of my business, I introduce my clients to the web designers early in the process of creating their site. I do this by copying everyone on an email message, giving information about each person on the email list. I also invite the client to contact the designer directly, rather than having to go through me for each detail.

This accomplishes several goals. First, my staff feels more a part of the business. So they take more ownership in their role in the business.

Next, it lets my client know that I'm not doing this alone. It gives them a great deal of comfort to know they can contact someone besides me – especially when they see my travel schedule!

Finally, it helps me turn over the responsibility to staff members, paving the way for my absence and for their taking more responsibility in the future.

List Resources

If you have a website that attracts your target audience, they are more likely to come back if they find quality content at your site. One way you can provide that is by creating a list of resources that relate to your area of expertise.

For example, if you are a music producer, you may want to have links to sites with products you've created, articles on how to produce music, sites where visitors can get music-related clip art, and sites for mp3 files that can be used royalty-free.

By being the source of quality information, your visitors are more likely to bookmark your site and revisit to see what is new. In addition, they'll recommend your site to their friends!

Show Your Affiliations

When you belong to organizations, you want to tell others about it. Generally, these affiliations are most appropriate on your "About our company" page.

Add logos and links to the organizations with whom you're affiliated. This may be the Better Business Bureau, the Chamber of Commerce, and other organizations.

Not only do your affiliations build your credibility, but they often provide the "link" between you and one of your prospects.

Tactic #68

Integrate Testimonials

One of the most effective sales techniques you can use is providing testimonials from satisfied customers. This is just as true online as offline. So start with the idea of the Congratulatory Wall where you display letters from your satisfied customers. Then move it to your website.

Because you don't know which page a visitor will see, it's a good idea to scatter testimonials throughout your site. They can be at the top of a page, within the contents of a page, or toward the bottom. The idea is to show your prospects what others have said about you and your business. It will make your new customers more comfortable in doing business with you.

Ask the Expert

Your website is a showcase to your expertise. Whether your content is plumbing or public speaking, you know more about it than your visitors. Show off that expertise by providing an Ask the Expert service.

On a page of your site, add a form to Ask the Expert. Require that the visitor provide their name and email address when they ask the question. It's best to use a form so you can specify the format and the information you want; however, you can use an email link if necessary.

When you get a question, respond directly to the person requesting the information. Then post the question and answer in your Expert column.

Change your Expert column frequently.

When you move a question off of the expert spotlight, add it to your FAQs (see Tactic #70).

When you first start your Ask the Expert column, it may be slow to start. To "seed" the questions, list the top ten questions you get repeatedly about your area of expertise. Then answer one question per week. That will get you started!

Post an FAQ

Frequently Asked Questions (FAQs) are a valuable part of your website. They provide a way for you to give your visitors valuable information in a condensed format.

There are several types of FAQs that you should have on your site. One is for your potential customers. What do they need to know about your product? Another is for your customers, after they have purchased. How can they use the product or service more effectively? Are there warranty issues that they must know about? A third FAQ is for your vendors. What do they need to know to do business with you?

Keep track of the questions that you get and add them to your FAQs. Your Ask the Expert questions and answers are one way to add to the FAQs. Another is looking at the service questions, phone questions, and support questions you and your staff receive.

Generally, the more information you put into your FAQs online, the fewer questions you'll need to answer personally!

Tactic #71

Provide Lots of Information

Your website can be another sales representative for you. It can answer the questions your clients have before they contact you, so that by the time they call or visit or sign up, they are ready to buy.

You want to provide enough information on your products and services that the buying decision is easy for your prospects. Your information may include brochures they can read online or download and print for offline use. Include a list of Frequently Asked Questions – with the answers. For starters, you will want to include information about your policies on shipping, returns, warranty, customer satisfaction, privacy, after-sales service, special offers, and the credit cards you accept.

An effective technique to identify the types of information you want to provide is to ask your staff members who answer the telephone or email messages from prospects and clients. In addition, call some of your prospects and newer clients and ask what types of questions they have or what type of information they want to see before making a buying decision. It is an excellent source of information and provides another excuse for your sales force to make contact with your prospects and customers.

Send Clippings

One of the best traditional ways to stay in touch with your clients is to send them articles that interest them. Generally, you'll add a note card or a yellow sticky saying "Thought this might interest you." Now you can do the same online.

When you find an article that would be helpful to a client, send the URL for the article to them in an email, telling them why you're sending it. They will appreciate your thoughtfulness, both in your sending the article and in your not enclosing the entire article. By providing a link, you leave it to their discretion as to when and if they click on the link to the article to read the entire article. Plus you do not overload their email box with unnecessary attachments.

You can send an article to an entire group of people, but remember to put their names in the BCC (blind carbon copy) field so that they cannot see who else you're sending it to. If they see they are part of a list, the tactic will lose its special, personalized appeal.

Empower Your Clients

Your satisfied clients are your best sales force. Nothing can sell a product or service faster than a personal recommendation from a satisfied customer. So you need to give them the tools they need to "sell you."

Early in the completed sales process, provide the wording you want them to use when describing you to others. It should be short and memorable. It should be something they can repeat easily and naturally to their friends. Put this in an email to them, perhaps even suggesting they recommend you to their friends, using the wording you have provided.

When giving a client a business card, give them two cards – one for them and one to pass on to a friend. It will give them the idea of sharing information about you.

When you give them literature, give them an extra copy to pass on to a friend.

When you give them a free sample, ask them for others who would like a free sample, too. Online, you can ask them to complete a "refer-a-friend" form, where they list the emails of their friends who will receive a short note automatically from your happy customer.

Continue to educate your clients about your business. Send them email updates on new products, new services, new successes. They will share in your excitement and tell others about you.

Set Expectations for Response

Time is compressed online. So while people used to be satisfied to get a letter within the week, online they expect an answer within the day. They prefer getting it the same day. But if they have to wait more than 24 hours, they're convinced you are either ignoring them or have gone out of business.

Make it a policy that everyone in your company will acknowledge all email messages within 4 hours of receiving them. This can be done with an autoresponder (Tactic #81). That will at least let the other person know you have received their email (a great fear among newer online users). Then try to respond with a full personalized answer within 24 hours.

If you adopt this policy, then put the policy on your contact forms. A simple "Expect to hear from us within 24 hours" will reassure those requesting more information.

On the other hand, if you do not plan to respond within 24 hours, tell them so that they are not upset when they do not get an answer within the time limit they prefer. A simple "We read all of your email; however, because of the volume of email that we receive, we will not respond directly" can go a long way to making your policy clear. Of course, a better statement (if you plan to abide by it) is "We read all of your email and try to respond within the week."

The important thing is to set the expectation and let the prospect know when, or if, they can anticipate an answer. It is unforgivable to ignore this issue.

Tactic #75

Exceed Expectations

Whether you are online or offline it is always a good policy to under-promise and over-deliver. But online it's even more important.

Because your online presence is not tangible to your clients and prospects, there may be an element of distrust. Providing extra levels of service helps to build your credibility and believability as a quality business. On the other hand, if you promise something and fail to fulfill it, it reinforces your customers' fears that you are not a "real" business.

As an example, promise delivery in 3 to 5 days, then ship via priority mail so that the package arrives in 1 to 2 days. Promise to follow up, then provide an extra report, a special gift or a series of emails that explain even more than your customer expected.

To tune into this attitude, ask "what else?"

They requested a brochure.
What else can I provide that would be helpful?
You might offer an email course or a teleseminar on the topic.

They requested a three-point analysis.
What else can I provide that would show our expertise and give them even more value?
Provide a five point analysis plus a special report.

Offer Polls and Surveys

Everyone loves being asked their opinion. Then they like to find out if their opinion matches everyone else's. So give them a chance!

Polls are short multiple choice questions that provide a quick way to gauge reactions. Generally polls provide immediate results so that after a website visitor answers, they can see how the answers are currently ranking. Polls can be generic or customized. In most cases, polls are only left on your website for a few days.

Surveys are longer than polls and usually appear on your site for a longer time. Since a survey is longer, you don't usually show the results. Instead, you can ask participants to provide their email address if they would like to see the results later. Surveys can be a valuable means of doing in-depth research, which can be reported in a special report.

Both polls and surveys are good ways to get input from your visitors. You can ask which topics they want more information on, which products they want to see developed, what price they think is appropriate for a specific product or service, or a variety of other questions.

Because they are interactive, visitors are more likely to return to your site to see the next poll or survey. You can send an email notice when you change the poll.

As an alternative you send a poll or survey via email and ask for responses in that format.

Tactic #77

Make Your Archives Accessible

If someone signs up for your ezine and likes it, they'll want to look at back issues. Sometimes they'll even want to look at back issues before they subscribe.

If your archives are online, you can refer to past articles in your newsletter. This gives readers the sense of longevity - and thereby builds your credibility!

On the other hand, you may want to limit the number of archives that you provide online. This would provide a reason to collect visitor information – so that you can send them the back issue.

Offer e-Lessons

An e-lesson is a short electronic lesson or online tutorial. It may be a how-to or a background lesson on a specific topic. Generally an e-lesson is only a page or two long.

e-Lessons are a good way to educate your prospects and customers, particularly if you have a complex business, such as insurance or finance. Likewise, if you have a product that can be used in different ways, e-lessons are helpful in showing them how to use their product beyond the basic functions.

e-Lessons vary in their complexity and technology. Some are simple web pages. Others are Adobe Acrobat PDF files. Still others are pages with audio or video instructions included.

Consider whether or not your audience will want to print the lesson before you determine which format to use. If they need the lesson next to them as they perform the task, then you'll want to stay with web pages or PDF files. Be sure either will print on a standard printer.

Tactic #79

Add Visual Appeal

Unless someone is reading a brief article or report, they generally need something to break up the line on a website. Computer screens create a line of text too wide to be read comfortably. Instead, you should create columns for your content. People read columns with more ease because they find the shorter lines more relaxing. To add visual interest, include graphics to break up those columns and improve the look of the page.

If you are creating a large page of content such as an electronic report or an ebook that you believe people will read online, use a 14-point or larger font with lots of white space on the page and between lines of text. This will make it easier and less tiring for your audience to read on the screen.

Photographs increase interest. When you look at a newspaper or a magazine, you automatically look at the photographs first, reading the captions below them, before you read the content on the page. People do the same thing on a website. So when possible include photographs of relevant topics and people with a caption underneath the photograph.

Tailor Your Website to Your Audience

There are many techniques you can use on your website to make it attractive to your audience. For example, if your target audience is people 50 and older, use a larger font size on your web pages rather than a smaller font. If your target audience are those 25 and below, provide brighter color and more interaction on your website. If your target audience is corporate America, use corporate colors such as grays, blues, maroons, and mauves.

Use the language of your target audience.

Design specific areas for different target audiences if your single website serves different audiences.

Know the types and speed of browsers that your audience uses. For example, if your target audience includes people at home, many of whom are using older computers with telephone connections, you won't want to include a lot of high-end graphics and movement on your site. On the other hand, if your target audience is a corporate audience using fast connections, you can include larger graphics and more complex interactions on the site.

Offer Autoresponders on Specific Topics

An autoresponder is an automatic reply to a specified email address. It can be as long as you want it to be.

The purpose of an autoresponder is to provide a quick answer to a common question. For example, many people inquire about our website design services. While we have a section on our website about this, sometimes it's easier to ask them to send an email to
website@TechTamers.com.
In response, they get a full-page email that outlines the process we use to create a website in four weeks.

This has several advantages. First, since this is a frequent question, it saves the time it would take to respond to every request for more information.

Second, if prospects had to wait for me to get back to the office to check email, then respond, they might get impatient and take their business elsewhere. Instead they send the email requesting the information and they get the answer by return email. It makes our company look very efficient!

Finally, I can compose a comprehensive answer once, then use it indefinitely. It's more likely to answer their questions because of the time taken initially with crafting the message, than if I had answered each request individually.

What questions do you get regularly? Are there autoresponders you need to create to provide better service for your prospects and customers?

Offer Multiple Contact Forms

Most web sites only have one contact form. On that single form they try to put everything anyone could ever ask for. Instead of a single form, consider providing a variety of contact forms for special purposes throughout your site.

You can have one contact form that targets those who want more information on your services. Another form could address those who want more information on specific products. In each area, target the information that you need and that your visitors will be most likely to request.

Direct the results of the forms to the appropriate people within the company. By sending the information to the person who is able to answer it most easily, you are able to deliver responses to your visitors more quickly and save staff time within your company.

Make it Easy to Print an Article

If you have laid out an article in such a way that it looks attractive on the web page, it is generally too wide to print on standard paper. While some people may read it online, others will choose to print the article to read offline or take with them.

Always provide a way to print the article in a printer-friendly format. To do this easily, just create another web page, leave off the graphics and the border. For the printer-friendly version, link from the attractive web page to this version that is just plain text with a heading and the URL at the bottom so they know where this particular article came from.

There are also scripts you can include on your articles that will automatically generate a printer-friendly version. Check with your webmaster for that information.

Tactic #84

Provide Case Studies

Everyone likes to read the story of success. By providing case studies on your website, in your ezine, or your other materials, you're giving your readers a way to identify with the success of others. This leads them to automatically want to achieve that success themselves. Take your client successes and write them up as case studies that will be applicable to your prospects.

Post case studies on your website and make them a part of your website. You can either have a special area for case studies or, if you have a case study that illustrates a particular topic in an article, you can have a link from that article to the case study. You could also highlight case studies within your ezine.

When possible, provide photos or illustrations within the case study. Specific details, such as organizational charts or diagrams of a process, make it more interesting to read and more realistic for your readers.

Offer an Email Course

Email courses are an easy way to offer information. You can offer a short course of only three to five lessons or a long-term course as long as 52 weeks with an email every week. The email message may be the lesson itself or it may point to a web page or an Adobe Acrobat PDF file.

Email courses are typically delivered via a sequential autoresponder. With this technology, you write each lesson, then schedule the frequency of lesson deliveries. The autoresponder engine tracks each person's enrollment and sends the appropriate message according to the schedule.

Email courses provide the advantage of delivery to the requestor's email box. So the course lessons may be more likely to be read than a full online course. Email courses are particularly effective when used to follow up leads, provide more information for the buying decision or teach a new customer to use the product more effectively.

Tactic #86

Offer Online Courses

If you truly want to show your expertise you can offer online courses. These can be as simple or as complex as you like.

Online courses offer the advantage of educating your audience. This is particularly critical if you have a complex product to sell. Insurance, for example, is an ideal business to offer an online course - on each type of insurance or on how to choose the best policy for you.

To start, offer short tutorials or e-lessons on your website so your audience can refer to them as needed.

Next, offer an email course of 5 to 7 lessons. This can be a bonus for signing up for one of your products or lists, or it can be the product itself.

When you've gained some experience, you can provide an online course using a course delivery system or through one of the online universities.

In some industries it may be more appropriate to offer a course using live interaction on the web. These work well when all attendees have a fast connection so voice and graphics can travel over the Internet while everyone is online. Many of these live presentations can be recorded for later playback.

Host a Teleseminar

A teleseminar is a group meeting via telephone. Because a standard telephone "bridge line" will hold up to 30 people for a teleseminar, this is similar to a large conference call. Each person calls into the bridge line, paying for their own long distance call. Most teleseminars last an hour or less.

Using a teleseminar is a good way to offer a "live" connection with visitors to your website. Teleseminars are an effective way to educate your prospects and to provide after-sale support for your customers. You can invite guest speakers to be interviewed on the seminar. Consider offering teleseminars as a paid service, too.

In addition to offering the teleseminars, which can only host 30 people, you should plan to record the seminar. You can offer the audiotapes as a product for sale on your site or you can send it to those seeking the information, free of charge.

Tactic #88

Offer Audios or Videos

With the advent of faster connections, many people are now able to listen to audio or watch video on their computers. This means you need to start considering what you could add to your site in either of those formats.

Audio is good for a voiceover while the visitor looks at pictures or slides. For example, you could tell someone how to use a feature of your product while they see pictures of the product. You could offer testimonials from satisfied customers via audio, with pictures of them shown on the screen. Because audio can run on slower connections, it's always good to provide it, even if you offer video as well.

Video can be a movie online. However, don't expect it to work flawlessly and look like a theater movie. Instead, use it for interviews or for action scenes that require motion. As you did with your audio, use it to show your customers how to use your product or service.

Always make audio or video an optional feature, so that viewers can choose whether or not they want to see it or listen to it at this time. If they are short of time or on a slower connection, they may choose not to click on it. Instead, provide a written transcript or article that provides the same information, without requiring the audio or video.

Tactic #89

Offer Audio and Video via CD

Some of your site visitors don't have fast connections. They won't click on a video or audio clip to listen or see it online. So if you want them to see the content that you've put into those formats, you'll need to provide it in a form they can use. Why not a CD?

They can order a CD and have it sent to them in the mail. Then they can view the content on their computer offline.

What types of content might you put on a CD? You can put an hour's audio or 15 minutes of video. You can add your entire website to the CD with barely a blink! Plus, you can offer additional forms, documents, articles, and other free information.

CDs are an excellent way to attract visitors to your site. By offering a free CD of information on a specific topic, many people will sign up for your email newsletter or a trial of your service. If you prefer, you can charge shipping on a free CD or actually sell the CD as a product.

Tactics to Build Your Expertise

If you're like most small business owners or managers, you're busy! There are never enough hours in the day. And if you've been doing this for a while, you are probably behind the learning curve in some areas. Managing your web site may be one of those areas.

When you see "manage your web site" don't think of technical, hands-on work. Instead, think of the business decisions that need to be made that will be reflected on your web site. You don't have to be the person to do the web work in order to be a good web manager.

Regardless of your level of involvement in the technical aspects of your web site, you need to start or continue your education on this important topic of doing business online. The tactics in this section include specific actions you can take to build your expertise in online success!

Learn to Manage Your Site

As the Internet developed there were people who took to the technical aspect of the medium and others who chose to ignore it – either through lack of time or interest. But if the Internet and your web site are to be an integral part of your business, you must learn enough about it to manage your online presence.

There are numerous ways to learn about your site. Look at it as a novice and ask the questions only novices think of. Then ask your technical guru or web designer to explain these things.

Next learn that anything is possible technically. However, it should be done only if you, the business owner or manager, asks for it. For example, a novice will often prefer simple navigation features like buttons and text links. However, people who love technology often prefer a more complex navigation system with fancy graphics that take longer to load. As the decision-maker, you should specify what you want your prospects and customers to see. You know them better than your technical staff does.

Continue to learn about your site. The Internet and technology in general change rapidly. The more you know the more you will recognize what you need to know. So keep learning!

Keep an Activity Log

As you start to make a series of changes, it is important that you track what you do and when you do it. Without this information, you are likely to forget that you added an ezine sign-up form on every page, which accounts for the jump in ezine subscribers you just experienced. Without an activity log, you will forget which search engines you've registered in and when you need to re-register .

At a minimum your activity log should include what you did, which websites or pages were involved, and the date you did it. You can maintain it electronically or by hand, but do maintain it!

Tactic #92

Attend Conferences and Seminars

Learning is a continuous process, particularly when you are working in an area that is new to you. This is particularly true in an online world, where things change faster than you can absorb them.

Conferences and seminars offer good learning experiences, both in the formal sessions and during the breaks. With effective networking you can form ongoing relationships with other attendees with similar businesses and online experience.

While face-to-face conferences and seminars have been the norm in the past, you will see an increasing number of online conferences and seminars you can attend. These offer the same information you'll see at a live conference, plus they save you travel time and costs. Online seminars and conferences can yield the same advantages of a "live" event, so look for them and try them out!

Subscribe to Publications

There are numerous online newsletters as well as offline publications that can help you build your expertise in how to use technology and the Internet. Talk to other business managers you know and ask what they read. Ask them to forward a copy of their favorite email newsletters to you so that you can see if you want to subscribe to those publications.

Collect What You Like

The Internet is a constantly changing landscape. Websites that were designed four years ago are now considered "old-fashioned." New strategies are constantly being developed. Your favorite sites change from one month to another.

Develop a system for keeping track of what you like. Generally, a notebook works well. When you find a web page whose design you like, print it and put it into the notebook. When you see a graphic or a specific format you like, print it and add it to the notebook. When you see a technique, such as cascading menus or rollover buttons, that you like, print it and add it to the notebook. When you see a good information presentation format, print it and add it to the notebook.

All of these collections will make your next web site revision painless. You can show your web designer what you like and leave it to them to determine how to implement it. It is much easier than starting from scratch to decide what you want on your site.

Find an Online Business Mentor

No matter how much you know about online techniques, there are always new items coming out that you need additional help with. You'll want to have somebody who knows a little more than you do but someone who can still explain it to you. This is someone you can email or call with your questions. Someone who understands your business well enough that they can explain the new technologies or new techniques in terms of your business.

When looking for an online business mentor, you will want to talk to your friends at a trade association, who are familiar with how your business operates. Talk to your business mastermind group or service group and see what others are doing online. You may find you want to have a variety of people you can call to get answers.

Form these relationships and treasure them because they are extremely valuable to you. They provide a measurable timesavings for the decision-making process you must follow to determine whether or not you want to adopt a new tactic or long-term strategy.

Find Someone You Can Mentor

It is said that we learn best by teaching. Most people will agree that when you understand something well enough that you can teach it to someone else, it helps organize that information within your own head. By doing that, you're not only consolidating information for yourself, but you are passing on the learning to those newer to online business.

Tactic #97

Find a Technical Mentor

Like any other profession, the technical area has some experts who are able and willing to communicate with novices, while other experts are unable or unwilling to take the time to explain complex concepts. The important thing is to find someone who will answer your questions in a way you understand.

No one was born with a chip in their head. Instead, all of us have had to go through the same learning experience. So there is always someone who is slightly ahead of you in the learning curve and someone who is behind you. Again, the important thing is to locate them.

Technical mentors are different than online business mentors. Technical mentors may not know anything about your business, but they do understand technology. With a technical mentor you can ask lots of small questions so you can clarify concepts. A good mentor can often explain both the technical and non-technical aspects of an issue, so that you can understand both sides.

When looking for a technical mentor do not rely only on professional relationships. Instead, look among your friends and acquaintances. They are often excited to be asked.

And remember to bring someone along behind you. It's true that you learn best by teaching. So take advantage of that and share the knowledge.

Perfect Techniques in the Background

"Not ready for prime time" is a good description for many web sites on the Internet today. They had a good idea, but they launched it too soon.

It is just as easy for you to build and experiment with a new tactic in the background as it is to do it in public. In order to do it in the background, you have your web designer (yes, it *can* be you!) create a new directory in your site. All of your work can be done in that directory. But since none of the pages in the directory link from any live pages, no one knows it's there except you.

This tactic is effective if you are planning to change the design of your site, if you want to try new graphics or new types of interaction, if you want to add a survey, or any other new item.

If you're starting to use a web-based service, such as an email management program, you can do this in the background as well, by using a limited number of recipients. These recipients should be people who understand you are in testing mode and who are willing to let you know what they are seeing. In this way, all of the bugs will be worked out before you involve the other 5,000 people on your email list!

Automate

One of the beauties of doing business online is that you can leverage the technology to help you automate many of the functions needed to be effective. Each time you perform a task ask if this is something you will do more than three times. If so, how can you automate it?

For example, if you get the same requests for information, put the information in an email and set it up as an autoresponder (Tactic #81) so that it goes out automatically when requested. Then add it to your Frequently Asked Questions document so that it is readily available at your web site.

Use an email management program when your email newsletter has more than 200 subscribers. A management program will handle all of the subscribes and unsubscribes, as well as the bounced email addresses. Many of them will allow you to compose and schedule your email newsletter weeks in advance of its distribution date.

Provide downloadable information, both on your web site and as products. With a downloadable ebook, for example, the customer completes the transaction and downloads their product – all without your intervention. You've marketed, sold, and delivered the product without lifting a finger!

Tactic #100

Complete One Step at a Time

One of the surest recipes for failure is to try to do it all at once. This is doubly true in online business, where you are often doing five different tasks that are all new to you.

Instead, map out the tactics you plan to use and put each on a timeline. While you can do two tasks at once, be sure that one of them is something you are already comfortable doing. Give yourself time to use, then measure the effectiveness of a tactic before going on to another.

While the online world provides the tools to do things quickly, until you are comfortable working at the speed of change, you are better off taking it one step at a time.

Take Action

No matter how many tactics can be written to build your business online, they are only effective when you take action and apply them. Decide today which three tactics you will tackle first. Implement those and measure your success. Then start on the next three.

Take Action Now!

About the Author

Jeanette S. Cates, PhD is the creator of the Online Success System and author of *Online Success System: a non-technical guide to managing your website.*

Dr. Cates is a frequent speaker at state and national conferences, with more than 200 presentations to her credit. Her fast-paced, information-packed presentations and her knack for explaining cutting-edge technology in easy-to-understand terms have gained her the reputation of being The Technology Tamer™.

As the owner of TechTamers she has developed a full line of learning materials, including more than 100 computer-based workshops, ranging from Basics of Operating System to Web-Page-in-a-Day™. She is a Certified Technical Trainer and is conversant with more than 200 software programs.

Dr. Cates holds a PhD in Instructional Design and Technology and an M.Ed. in Adult Education, both from the University of Texas at Austin. She earned a B.S. in Business Administration from Trinity University. She is listed in Who's Who of American Women and is a member of Women in Technology International and the National Speakers Association. Jeanette has been featured in PC World and Computer Shopper, among other technology-related publications. She is a regular contributor to wz.com and workz.com, as well as smallbusiness.com.

Jeanette has been married for over 32 years to Bob Cates, an Internal Auditor. They have three daughters – Stephanie, Jennifer and Vicki, and one grandson, J.R. – and another on the way!

About TechTamers

TechTamers is a consulting and training firm, based in Austin, Texas. Founded by Dr. Jeanette Cates, TechTamers works with organizations who want to reap the rewards of their online technology and with professionals who want to cut their technology learning curve. Visit TechTamers online at TechTamers.com or contact us at 512-219-5653.

Where to Find More Information

If you've been working through the tactics in this book, you may want to expand your knowledge and get more details on some of them.

The first place to start is with good questions. Here are some suggestions for questions you can ask when you are considering a specific tactic:

1. What online resources do I have to research this tactic in more detail?

2. Who might be able to provide me with the resources I need to implement this tactic?

3. How long would it take me to implement this tactic?

4. Where does this fit into my overall strategy for my online presence?

5. When do I want to make this goal a reality?

Here are six ways you can take your tactics to the next level.

1. Go to the OnlineSuccessTactics.com web site. Remember to send an email requesting the password to updates@OnlineSuccessTactics.com so that you will be able to log into the private area of the site. In that area you'll find additional information on most of the tactics in the book. You'll find links to online articles, tutorials, and books on the tactic.

2. Go to the OnlineBusinessMastery.com web site. This is the main web site for the series of books of which Online $uccess Tactics is a part. The series includes over 100 strategies that explain the tactics in more detail, plus online resources to support the strategies.

3. Go to your local bookstore and browse the shelves in the Small Business and Web site sections. You'll find other great books that can help you go one step further with your online business.

4. Check with your local community college to see what courses they offer in the area of web sites and online business. You'll probably find other learners in those courses with whom you can continue to learn, long after the class has ended.

5. Look for online courses on the topic. There are a growing number of courses that can meet your needs. As with face-to-face courses, you'll form a support group whose value will last long after the course has concluded.

6. Participate in one of the Coaching for Online Success programs offered through TechTamers. Check at TechCoach.net for the current programs enrolling new participants.

Finally, email me (cates@TechTamers.com) with your questions and comments. It will make the next edition even better and will provide better content for the Web-Enhanced site. Plus, I'd love to hear about your successes as you use the Online $uccess Tactics!

Glossary

Affiliate programs – a program to establish, support and reward an outside sales force. By joining an affiliate program, you have the right to refer your visitors to a specific site where they might purchase a product. When they purchase, you earn an affiliate commission. Likewise, you can establish an affiliate program for your site and products and pay referral fees (commissions) to those who sign up for your program.

Autoresponder – an automatic response sent via email. Autoresponders are used to send quick responses to queries that you receive regularly. To create an autoresponder, you write the email message you want sent. Then you load that message into a program that will automatically send the message each time it receives an email. For example, send an email to website@TechTamers.com and you will receive an autoresponder reply.

Contact form – a form to be filled in by the visitor. When they click the Submit button the information is sent to your contact's email address. Typically you have at least one contact form on your web site or you may have several with different purposes. The advantage of using a form over a simple email link is that a form guides the visitor as to the information you need to provide an appropriate response.

Discussion list – an online message board where visitors can post messages and respond to other messages. Discussion lists are asynchronous – that is not everyone has to be online at the same time. Instead, questions and replies are posted whenever someone visits the board.

Domain name – the name given to your website in its address. Your domain name may be the same name as your company (TechTamers' site is TechTamers.com) or it may be totally different (OnlineSuccessTactics.com is a domain owned by TechTamers).

Email newsletter – a newsletter sent via email. Newsletters are often sent to an in-house list and may be more casual than an ezine. And whereas an ezine may contain advertising, newsletters are often ad-free. However, in common use, the ezine and email newsletter are often used interchangeably.

Ezine – Electronic magazine. This term often is more applicable than email newsletter. Whereas a newsletter is often ad-free and considered an in-house publication, an ezine is expected to contain both information and advertising. However, in common use, the ezine and email newsletter are often used interchangeably.

FAQ – Frequently Asked Questions. This a page of questions, with their answers. You can place an FAQ within the sales area, the customer service area or any other place where you typically receive questions.

Home page – the first page that your visitor sees. The actual title of the page may be anything. The file name for the home page varies, depending on the server you are using for your web site host. So it may be index.html or default.html.

Sequential Autoresponder – a series of emails sent automatically. The series is triggered with the first email received by the designated address. Sequential autoresponders are an excellent method to follow up leads, to provide product information over a period of time, to send a series of tips on how to use a newly purchased product and even to deliver a short course. To create a sequential autoresponder series, you create the emails, put them into the autoresponder engine, then schedule them for specified intervals. To see an example, send an email to elearning@TechTamers.com and you'll receive a 7-lesson series on elearning.

Signature file – a file added to the end of your email message. Your signature file should contain your name, web site and any ways that you want to be contacted (phone, fax, email, physical address). You can also add advertising information to your signature file. You can have a variety of signature files that you use for different purposes and different audiences. See the help file in your email program to see how to set up a signature file.

Specialty items – small give-away items with your logo and message on them. This can range from t-shirts to bumper stickers to coffee mugs to pens to key chains.

Teleseminar – a telephone seminar. Each attendee, as well as the presenters, call into a telephone bridge line. They are then connected and able to converse as they usually do with a conference call. On some of the more sophisticated bridge lines, the presenters can mute the audience for a period.

URL – this is the web address you give someone to find your site in general or a specific page within the site. For example, Tech4Speakers.com is the URL for the site and will take you to the front page (home page) of that site. Tech4Speakers.com/store/ is the URL for a section within the site and will take you directly to that section. Tech4Speakers.com/store/onlinepresence.htm will take you to the section then to a specific page within that section. Many URLs nowadays do not require the http:// in front of them and most do not require the www.

Virtual trade show – an online version of the traditional trade show. Depending on the service that hosts the show, it may contain virtual booths, a badge scanner, photos of products, links to the advertiser's web site, audio, video, and other media that simulate a regular trade show.

Web site or website – the collection of pages that comprise all of your information online at a single address. You can have multiple websites.

Index

Websites Mentioned

Bonu$

As a valued customer of *Online Success Tactics*, we would like to offer a free website tune-up course. In multiple lessons you'll have the opportunity to look at your website from your target audience's perspective.

To enroll in the free course on Seven Secrets to a Better Website, send an email to 7secrets@TechTamers.com.

Quick Order Form

Online: http://www.TwinTowersPress.com. Ebook versions available.

Fax orders: (512) 219-5654. Send this form.

Telephone orders: Call toll-free 877-522-8371 with your credit card.
512-219-5653
Email orders: orders@TwinTowersPress.com

Postal orders: Twin Towers Press, 10502 Hardrock, Austin, TX 78750-2037, USA.

Please send the following books. I understand that I may return any item for a full refund – no questions asked.

- ❏ Online Success Tactics: Top 100 Ways to Build your Small Business, $14.95
- ❏ Online Success System: a non-technical guide to managing your website, $29.95
- ❏ Online Success Strategies for Visibility, $39.95
- ❏ Online Success Strategies for Sales, $39.95
- ❏ Online Success Strategies for Support, $39.95

Name ————————————————————————————

Address ——————————————————————————

City ————————— State ———— Zip ———— - ————

Telephone ———————————————————————————

Email address———————————————————————————

Sales tax: Please add 8.25% for products shipped to Texas addresses.

Shipping to the U.S. $3 per book
International: $9 for first book; $5 for each additional (estimate)

Payment: ❏ Check   ❏ Credit Card (MasterCard, Visa, Amex)

Card Number: ——————————————————————

Name on Card: ———————— Exp. Date: ——— / ———

Notes

Quick Order Form

Online: http://www.TwinTowersPress.com. Ebook versions available.

Fax orders: (512) 219-5654. Send this form.

Telephone orders: Call toll-free 877-522-8371 with your credit card.

Email orders: orders@TwinTowersPress.com

Postal orders: Twin Towers Press, 10502 Hardrock, Austin, TX 78750-2037, USA.

Please send the following books. I understand that I may return any item for a full refund – no questions asked.

❑   Online Success Tactics: Top 100 Ways to Build your Small Business, $14.95

❑   Online Success System: a non-technical guide to managing your website, $29.95

❑   Online Success Strategies for Visibility, $39.95

❑   Online Success Strategies for Sales, $39.95

❑   Online Success Strategies for Support, $39.95

Name _____

Address _____

City _____ State _____ Zip _____ - _____

Telephone _____

Email address _____

Sales tax: Please add 8.25% for products shipped to Texas addresses.

Shipping to the U.S. $3 per book
International: $9 for first book; $5 for each additional (estimate)

Payment: ❑ Check   ❑ Credit Card (MasterCard, Visa, Amex)

Card Number: _____

Name on Card: _____ Exp. Date: _____ / _____

Notes